THE STANZAS OF DZYAN.

(From "The Secret Doctrine.")

TRANSLATED BY H. P. B. ∴

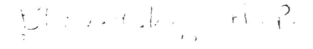

Printed on the H. P. B. Press.

1892.

COSMIC EVOLUTION.

———

STANZA I.

1. The Eternal Parent, wrapped in her Ever-Invisible Robes, had slumbered once again for Seven Eternities.

2. Time was not, for it lay asleep in the Infinite Bosom of Duration.

3. Universal Mind was not, for there were no Ah-hi to contain it.

4. The Seven Ways to Bliss were not. The Great Causes of Misery were not, for there was no one to produce and get ensnared by them.

5. Darkness alone filled the Boundless All, for Father, Mother and Son were once more one, and the Son had not yet awakened for the new Wheel and his Pilgrimage thereon.

6. The Seven Sublime Lords and the Seven Truths had ceased to be, and the Universe, the Son of Necessity, was

immersed in Paranishpanna, to be outbreathed by that which is, and yet is not. Naught was.

7. The Causes of Existence had been done away with; the Visible that was, and the Invisible that is, rested in Eternal Non-Being—the One Being.

8. Alone, the One Form of Existence stretched boundless, infinite, causeless, in Dreamless Sleep; and Life pulsated unconscious in Universal Space, throughout that All-Presence, which is sensed by the Opened Eye of Dangma.

9. But where was Dangma when the Âlaya of the Universe was in Paramârtha, and the Great Wheel was Anupâdaka?

Stanza II.

1. . . . Where were the Builders, the Luminous Sons of Manvantaric Dawn? . . . In the Unknown Darkness in their Ah-hi Paranishpanna. The Producers of Form from No-Form—the Root of the World—the Devâmatri and Svabhâvat, rested in the Bliss of Non-Being.

2. . . . Where was Silence? Where the ears to sense it? No, there was neither Silence nor Sound; naught save Ceaseless Eternal Breath, which knows itself not.

3. The Hour had not yet struck; the Ray had not yet flashed into the Germ; the Mâtripadma had not yet swollen.

4. Her Heart had not yet opened for the One Ray to enter, thence to fall, as Three into Four, into the Lap of Mâyâ.

5. The Seven were not yet born from the Web of Light. Darkness alone was Father-Mother, Svabhâvat; and Svabhâvat was in Darkness.

6. These Two are the Germ, and the Germ is One. The Universe was still concealed in the Divine Thought and the Divine Bosom.

Stanza III.

1. . . . . The last Vibration of the Seventh Eternity thrills through Infinitude. The Mother swells, expanding from within without, like the Bud of the Lotus.

2. The Vibration sweeps along, touching with its swift Wing the whole Universe and the Germ that dwelleth in Darkness, the Darkness that breathes over the slumbering Waters of Life.

3. Darkness radiates Light, and Light drops one solitary Ray into the Waters, into the Mother-Deep. The Ray shoots

through the Virgin Egg, the Ray causes the Eternal Egg to thrill, and drop the non-eternal Germ, which condenses into the World-Egg.

4. The Three fall into the Four. The Radiant Essence becomes Seven inside, Seven outside. The Luminous Egg, which in itself is Three, curdles and spreads in milk-white Curds throughout the Depths of Mother, the Root that grows in the Depths of the Ocean of Life.

5. The Root remains, the Light remains, the Curds remain, and still Oeaohoo is One.

6. The Root of Life was in every Drop of the Ocean of Immortality, and the Ocean was Radiant Light, which was Fire, and Heat, and Motion. Darkness vanished and was no more; it disappeared in its own Essence, the Body of Fire and Water, of Father and Mother.

7. Behold, O Lanoo, the Radiant Child of the Two, the unparalleled refulgent Glory—Bright Space, Son of Dark Space, who emerges from the Depths of the great Dark Waters. It is Oeaohoo, the Younger, the * * *. He shines forth as the Sun, he is the Blazing Divine Dragon of Wisdom; the Eka is Chatur, and Chatur takes to itself Tri, and the Union produces the

Sapta, in whom are the Seven, which become the Tridasha, the Hosts and the Multitudes. Behold him lifting the Veil, and unfurling it from East to West. He shuts out the Above, and leaves the Below to be seen as the Great Illusion. He marks the places for the Shining Ones, and turns the Upper into a shoreless Sea of Fire, and the One Manifested into the Great Waters.

8. Where was the Germ, and where was now Darkness? Where is the Spirit of the Flame that burns in thy Lamp, O Lanoo? The Germ is That, and That is Light, the White Brilliant Son of the Dark Hidden Father.

9. Light is Cold Flame, and Flame is Fire, and Fire produces Heat, which yields Water—the Water of Life in the Great Mother.

10. Father-Mother spin a Web, whose upper end is fastened to Spirit, the Light of the One Darkness, and the lower one to its shadowy end, Matter; and this Web is the Universe, spun out of the Two Substances made in One, which is Svabhâvat.

11. It expands when the Breath of Fire is upon it; it contracts when the Breath of the Mother touches it. Then the Sons dissociate and scatter, to return into their Mother's Bosom,

at the end of the Great Day, and re-become one with her. When it is cooling, it becomes radiant. Its Sons expand and contract through their own Selves and Hearts; they embrace Infinitude.

12. Then Svabhâvat sends Fohat to harden the Atoms. Each is a part of the Web. Reflecting the "Self-Existent Lord," like a Mirror, each becomes in turn a World.

STANZA IV.

1. . . . Listen, ye Sons of the Earth, to your Instructors—the Sons of the Fire. Learn, there is neither first nor last; for all is One Number, issued from No-Number.

2. Learn what we, who descend from the Primordial Seven, we, who are born from the Primordial Flame, have learnt from our Fathers. . . .

3. From the Effulgency of Light—the Ray of the Ever-Darkness—sprang in Space the reäwakened Energies; the One from the Egg, the Six, and the Five.   Then the Three, the One, the Four, the One, the Five—the Twice Seven, the Sum Total. And these are the Essences, the Flames, the Elements, the Builders, the Numbers, the Arûpa, the Rûpa, and the Force or Divine Man, the Sum Total.   And from the Divine Man eman-

ated the Forms, the Sparks, the Sacred Animals, and the Messengers of the Sacred Fathers within the Holy Four.

4. This was the Army of the Voice, the Divine Mother of the Seven. The Sparks of the Seven are subject to, and the servants of, the First, the Second, the Third, the Fourth, the Fifth, the Sixth, and the Seventh of the Seven. These are called Spheres, Triangles, Cubes, Lines and Modellers; for thus stands the Eternal Nidâna—the Oi-Ha-Hou.

5. The Oi-Ha-Hou, which is Darkness, the Boundless, or the No-Number, Âdi-Nidâna Svabhâvat, the ◯ :

I. The Âdi-Sanat, the Number, for he is One.

II. The Voice of the Word, Svabhâvat, the Numbers, for he is One and Nine.

III. The "Formless Square."

And these Three, enclosed within the ◯, are the Sacred Four; and the Ten are the Arûpa Universe. Then come the Sons, the Seven Fighters, the One, the Eighth left out, and his Breath which is the Light-Maker.

6. . .∴. Then the Second Seven, who are the Lipika, produced by the Three. The Rejected Son is One. The "Son-Suns" are countless.

1. The Primordial Seven, the First Seven Breaths of the Dragon of Wisdom, produce in their turn from their Holy Circumgyrating Breaths the Fiery Whirlwind.

2. They make of him the Messenger of their Will. The Dzyu becomes Fohat: the swift Son of the Divine Sons, whose Sons are the Lipika, runs circular errands. Fohat is the Steed, and the Thought is the Rider. He passes like lightning through the fiery clouds; takes Three, and Five, and Seven Strides through the Seven Regions above, and the Seven below. He

lifts his Voice, and calls the innumerable Sparks, and joins them together.

3. He is their guiding spirit and leader. When he commences work, he separates the Sparks of the Lower Kingdom, that float and thrill with joy in their radiant dwellings, and forms therewith the Germs of Wheels. He places them in the Six Directions of Space, and One in the middle—the Central Wheel.

4. Fohat traces spiral lines to unite the Sixth to the Seventh—the Crown. An Army of the Sons of Light stands ,

at each angle; the Lipika, in the Middle Wheel. They say: "This is good." The first Divine World is ready; the First, the Second. Then the "Divine Arûpa" reflects itself in Chhâyâ Loka, the First Garment of Anupâdaka.

5. Fohat takes five strides, and builds a winged wheel at each corner of the square for the Four Holy Ones . . . and their Armies.

6. The Lipika circumscribe the Triangle, the First One, the Cube, the Second One, and the Pentacle within the Egg. It is the Ring called "Pass Not" for those who descend and

ascend; who during the Kalpa are progressing towards the Great Day "Be With Us." . . . Thus were formed the Arûpa and the Rûpa: from One Light, Seven Lights; from each of the Seven, seven times Seven Lights. The Wheels watch the Ring. . . .

———

Stanza VI.

1. By the power of the Mother of Mercy and Knowledge, Kwan-Yin—the Triple of Kwan-Shai-Yin, residing in Kwan-Yin-Tien—Fohat, the Breath of their Progeny, the Son of the

Sons, having called forth, from the lower Abyss, the Illusive Form of Sien-Tchan and the Seven Elements.

2. The Swift and the Radiant One produces the seven Laya Centres, against which none will prevail to the Great Day " Be With Us"; and seats the Universe on these Eternal Foundations, surrounding Sien-Tchan with the Elementary Germs.

3. Of the Seven—first One manifested, Six concealed ; Two manifested, Five concealed ; Three manifested, Four concealed ; Four produced, Three hidden ; Four and One Tsan revealed,

Two and One-Half concealed; Six to be manifested, One laid aside. Lastly, Seven Small Wheels revolving; one giving birth to the other.

4. He builds them in the likeness of older Wheels, placing them on the Imperishable Centres.

How does Fohat build them? He collects the Fiery-Dust. He makes Balls of Fire, runs through them, and round them, infusing life thereinto, then sets them into motion; some one way, some the other way. They are cold, he makes them hot. They are dry, he makes them moist. They shine, he fans and cools them. Thus acts Fohat from one Twilight to the other, during Seven Eternities.

5. At the Fourth, the Sons are told to create their Images. One-Third refuses. Two obey.

The Curse is pronounced. They will be born in the Fourth, suffer and cause suffering. This is the First War.

6. The Older Wheels rotated downward and upward. . . . The Mother's Spawn filled the whole. There were Battles fought between the Creators and the Destroyers, and Battles

fought for Space; the Seed appearing and reäppearing continuously.

7. Make thy calculations, O Lanoo, if thou wouldst learn the correct age of thy Small Wheel. Its Fourth Spoke is our Mother. Reach the Fourth Fruit of the Fourth Path of Knowledge that leads to Nirvâna, and thou shalt comprehend, for thou shalt see. . . .

———

STANZA VII.

1. Behold the beginning of sentient formless Life.
First, the Divine, the One from the Mother-Spirit; then, the

Spiritual; the Three from the One, the Four from the One, and the Five, from which the Three, the Five and the Seven. These are the Three-fold and the Four-fold downward; the Mind-born Sons of the First Lord, the Shining Seven. It is they who are thou, I, he, O Lanoo; they who watch over thee and thy mother, Bhûmi.

2. The One Ray multiplies the smaller Rays. Life precedes Form, and Life survives the last atom. Through the countless Rays the Life-Ray, the One, like a Thread through many Beads.

3. When the One becomes Two, the Threefold appears, and

the Three are One; and it is our Thread, O Lanoo, the Heart of the Man-Plant called Saptaparna.

4. It is the Root that never dies; the Three-tongued Flame of the Four Wicks. The Wicks are the Sparks, that draw from the Three-tongued Flame shot out by the Seven—their Flame—the Beams and Sparks of one Moon reflected in the running Waves of all the Rivers of Earth.

5. The Spark hangs from the Flame by the finest thread of Fohat. It journeys through the Seven Worlds of Mâyâ. It stops in the First, and is a Metal and a Stone; it passes into the

Second, and behold—a Plant; the Plant whirls through seven changes and becomes a Sacred Animal. From the combined attributes of these, Manu, the Thinker, is formed. Who forms him? The Seven Lives and the One Life. Who completes him? The Fivefold Lha. And who perfects the last Body? Fish, Sin, and Soma. . . .

6. From the First-born the Thread between the Silent Watcher and his Shadow becomes more strong and radiant with every Change. The morning Sunlight has changed into noon-day glory. . . .

7. "This is thy present Wheel," said the Flame to the Spark. "Thou art myself, my image and my shadow. I have clothed myself in thee, and thou art my Vâhan to the Day 'Be With Us,' when thou shalt re-become myself and others, thyself and me." Then the Builders, having donned their first Clothing, descend on radiant Earth and reign over Men—who are themselves. . . .

ANTHROPOGENESIS.

STANZA I.

1. The Lha which turns the Fourth is Servant to the Lha(s) of the Seven, they who revolve, driving their Chariots around their Lord, the One Eye of our World. His Breath gave Life to the Seven. It gave Life to the First.

2. Said the Earth: "Lord of the Shining Face, my House is empty. . . . . . Send thy Sons to people this Wheel.

Thou hast sent thy Seven Sons to the Lord of Wisdom. Seven times doth he see thee nearer to himself, seven times more doth he feel thee. Thou hast forbidden thy Servants, the small Rings, to catch thy Light and Heat, thy great Bounty to intercept on its passage. Send now to thy Servant the same."

3. Said the Lord of the Shining Face: "I shall send thee a Fire when thy work is commenced. Raise thy voice to other Lokas; apply to thy Father, the Lord of the Lotus, for his Sons. . . . . Thy People shall be under the rule

of the Fathers. Thy Men shall be mortals. The Men of the Lord of Wisdom, not the Sons of Soma, are immortal. Cease thy complaints. Thy Seven Skins are yet on thee. . . Thou art not ready. Thy Men are not ready."

4. After great throes she cast off her old Three and put on her new Seven Skins, and stood in her first one.

STANZA II.

5. The Wheel whirled for thirty crores more. It constructed Rûpas; soft Stones that hardened, hard Plants that

softened.   Visible from invisible, Insects and small Lives. She shook them off her back whenever they overran the Mother. . . . . After thirty crores, she turned round. She lay on her back; on her side. . . . She would call no Sons of Heaven, she would ask no Sons of Wisdom. She created from her own Bosom. She evolved Water-Men, terrible and bad.

6. The Water-Men, terrible and bad, she herself created from the remains of others.   From the dross and slime of her First, Second, and Third, she formed them.   The Dhyâni

came and looked . . . the Dhyani from the bright Father-Mother, from the White Regions they came, from the Abodes of the Immortal Mortals.

7. Displeased they were. "Our Flesh is not there. No fit Rûpas for our Brothers of the Fifth. No Dwellings for the Lives. Pure Waters, not turbid, they must drink. Let us dry them."

8. The Flames came. The Fires with the Sparks; the Night-Fires and the Day-Fires. They dried out the turbid dark Waters. With their heat they quenched them. The

Lhas of the High, the Lhamayin of Below, came. They slew the Forms which were two- and four-faced. They fought the Goat-Men, and the Dog-Headed Men, and the Men with fishes' bodies.

9. Mother-Water, the Great Sea, wept. She arose, she disappeared in the Moon, which had lifted her, which had given her birth.

10. When they were destroyed, Mother Earth remained bare. She asked to be dried.

Stanza III.

11. The Lord of the Lords came. From her Body he separated the Waters, and that was Heaven above, the First Heaven.

12. The great Chohans called the Lords of the Moon, of the Airy Bodies: "Bring forth Men, Men of your nature. Give them their Forms within. She will build Coverings without. Males-Females will they be. Lords of the Flame also. . . . ."

13. They went each on his allotted Land; Seven of them, each on his Lot. The Lords of the Flame remain behind. They would not go, they would not create.

———

Stanza IV.

14. The Seven Hosts, the Will-Born Lords, propelled by the Spirit of Life-Giving, separate Men from themselves, each on his own Zone.

15. Seven times seven Shadows of Future Men were born, each of his own Colour and Kind. Each inferior to his Father.

The Fathers, the Boneless, could give no Life to Beings with Bones. Their progeny were Bhûta, with neither Form nor Mind. Therefore they are called the Chhâyâ Race.

16. How are the Manushya born? The Manus with minds, how are they made? The Fathers called to their help their own Fire, which is the Fire that burns in Earth. The Spirit of the Earth called to his help the Solar Fire. These Three produced in their joint efforts a good Rûpa. It could stand, walk, run, recline, or fly. Yet it was still but a Chhâyâ, a Shadow with no Sense. . . .

17. The Breath needed a Form; the Fathers gave it. The

Breath needed a Gross Body; the Earth moulded it. The Breath needed the Spirit of Life; the Solar Lhas breathed it into its Form. The Breath needed a Mirror of its Body; "We gave it our own!"—said the Dhyânis. The Breath needed a Vehicle of Desires; "It has it!"—said the Drainer of Waters. But Breath needs a Mind to embrace the Universe; "We cannot give that!"—said the Fathers. "I never had it!"—said the Spirit of the Earth. "The Form would be consumed were I to give it mine!"—said the Great Fire. . . . Man remained an empty senseless Bhûta. . . . . Thus have the Boneless given Life to those who became Men with Bones in the Third.

18. The First were the Sons of Yoga. Their sons, the children of the Yellow Father and the White Mother.

19. The Second Race was the product by budding and expansion, the A-sexual from the Sexless. Thus was, O Lanoo, the Second Race produced.

20. Their Fathers were the Self-born. The Self-born, the Chhâyâ from the brilliant Bodies of the Lords, the Fathers, the Sons of Twilight.

21. When the Race became old, the old Waters mixed with the fresher Waters. When its Drops became turbid, they vanished and disappeared in the new Stream, in the hot Stream of Life. The Outer of the First became the Inner of the Second. The old Wing became the new Shadow, and the Shadow of the Wing.

———

STANZA VI.

22. Then the Second evolved the Egg-born, the Third. The Sweat grew, its Drops grew, and the Drops became hard

and round. The Sun warmed it; the Moon cooled and shaped it; the Wind fed it until its ripeness. The White Swan from the Starry Vault overshadowed the big Drop. The Egg of the Future Race, the Man-swan of the later Third. First male-female, then man and woman.

23. The Self-born were the Chhâyâs, the Shadows from the Bodies of the Sons of Twilight. Neither water nor fire could destroy them. Their sons were.

Stanza VII.

24. The Sons of Wisdom, the Sons of Night, ready for

rebirth, came down. They saw the vile forms of the First Third. "We can choose," said the Lords, "we have wisdom." Some entered the Chhâyâs. Some projected a Spark. Some deferred till the Fourth. From their own Rûpa they filled the Kâma. Those who entered became Arhats. Those who received but a Spark, remained destitute of knowledge; the Spark burned low. The Third remained mind-less. Their Jivas were not ready. These were set apart among the Seven. They became narrow-headed. The Third were ready. "In these shall we dwell," said the Lords of the Flame and of the Dark Wisdom.

25. How did the Manasa, the Sons of Wisdom, act? They rejected the Self-born. They are not ready. They spurned the Sweat-born. They are not quite ready. They would not enter the first Egg-born.

26. When the Sweat-born produced the Egg-born, the twofold, the mighty, the powerful with bones, the Lords of Wisdom said: "Now shall we create."

27. The Third Race became the Vâhan of the Lords of Wisdom. It created Sons of Will and Yoga, by Kriyashakti it created them, the Holy Fathers, Ancestors of the Arhats. . . .

STANZA VIII.

28. From the drops of sweat, from the residue of the substance, matter from dead bodies of men and animals of the Wheel before, and from cast-off dust, the first animals were produced.

29. Animals with bones, dragons of the deep, and flying Sarpas were added to the creeping things. They that creep on the ground got wings. They of the long necks in the water became the progenitors of the fowls of the air.

30. During the Third, the boneless animals grew and changed; they became animals with bones, their Chhâyâs became solid.

31. The animals separated the first. They began to breed. The two-fold man separated also. He said: "Let us as they; let us unite and make creatures." They did . . . .

32. And those which had no Spark took huge she-animals unto them. They begat upon them dumb races. Dumb they were themselves. But their tongues untied. The tongues of their progeny remained still. Monsters they

bred. A race of crooked red-hair-covered monsters going on all fours. A dumb race to keep the shame untold.

Stanza IX.

33. Seeing which, the Lhas who had not built men, wept, saying:

34. "The Amanasa have defiled our future abodes. This is Karma. Let us dwell in the others. Let us teach them better, lest worse should happen. They did . . . .

35. Then all men became endowed with Manas. They saw the sin of the mindless.

36. The Fourth Race developed speech.

37. The one became two; also all the living and creeping things that were still one, giant fish, birds and serpents with shell-heads.

Stanza X.

38. Thus, two by two, on the seven Zones, the Third Race gave birth to the Fourth; the Sura became A-sura.

39. The First, on every Zone, was moon-coloured; the Second yellow like gold; the Third red; the Fourth brown, which became black with sin. The first seven human shoots were all of one complexion. The next seven began mixing.

40. Then the Third and Fourth became tall with pride. "We are the kings; we are the gods."

41. They took wives fair to look upon. Wives from the mindless, the narrow-headed. They bred monsters, wicked demons, male and female, also Khado, with little minds.

42. They built temples for the human body. Male and female they worshipped. Then the Third Eye acted no longer.

STANZA XI.

43. They built huge cities. Of rare earths and metals they built. Out of the fires vomited, out of the white stone of the mountains and of the black stone, they cut their own images, in their size and likeness, and worshipped them.

44. They built great images nine yatis high, the size of their bodies. Inner fires had destroyed the land of their fathers. The water threatened the Fourth.

45. The first great waters came. They swallowed the seven great islands.

46. All holy saved, the unholy destroyed. With them most of the huge animals, produced from the sweat of the earth.

STANZA XII.

47. Few remained. Some yellow, some brown and black,

and some red remained.   The moon-coloured were gone
for ever.

48. The Fifth produced from the holy stock remained; it
was ruled over by the first Divine Kings.

49. . . . . The Serpents who re-descended, who made
peace with the Fifth, who taught and instructed it. . . .

Milton Keynes UK
Ingram Content Group UK Ltd.
UKHW020722131123
432470UK00011B/675

9 781015 402380